ROCKIN' STRINGS

T0066488

IMPROV LESSONS & TIPS FOR THE CONTEMPORARY PLAYER

BY MARK WOOD

FOREWORD BY DR. ROBERT GILLESPIE

To access audio online, visit:
www.halleonard.com/mylibrary

7050-5751-0222-4787

PLAYBACK+
Speed • Pitch • Balance • Loop

Cover art by Albert Oh

All music composed and performed by Mark Wood.

Mark Wood – 7-string Viper violin
Elijah Wood – drums
Rob Bambach – guitar
Paul Ranieri – bass

ISBN 978-1-4950-7177-5

Visit Hal Leonard Online at
www.halleonard.com

World headquarters, contact:
Hal Leonard
7777 West Bluemound Road
Milwaukee, WI 53213
Email: info@halleonard.com

In Europe, contact:
Hal Leonard Europe Limited
1 Red Place
London, W1K 6PL
Email: info@halleonardeurope.com

In Australia, contact:
Hal Leonard Australia Pty. Ltd.
4 Lentara Court
Cheltenham, Victoria, 3192 Australia
Email: info@halleonard.com.au

CONTENTS

ABOUT THE ONLINE AUDIO

On page 1 of this book you will find a code that allows you to access the online audio tracks. You can listen to these online or download them to your computer and/or mobile device. To hear a given etude, refer to its number; the online audio track is named accordingly (e.g., Etude 21 = Track 21).

The tracks for "Night Rider" and five additional play-along tracks are given below.

PLAY-ALONG TRACKS

TRACK 176 • **Night Rider** (demo)

TRACK 177 • **Night Rider** (play-along)

TRACK 178 • **Flying in D**

TRACK 179 • **Flying in G**

TRACK 180 • **Flying in C**

TRACK 181 • **Flying in A**

TRACK 182 • **Learning to Fly in D**

FOREWORD

Welcome to *Rockin' Strings*! Here is the chance to enter the new world of playing today's music while learning to express your own music through improvisation. Don't be afraid! *Rockin' Strings* is going to lead you step-by-step. We begin at home with the D major scale and then teach you how to create your own melodies and tunes one step at a time. Play along with the accompanying audio tracks. They will make you sound like a star as you begin to progress through the book, exploring additional keys and rhythms while improvising – all in the style of popular music. Play by yourself, with your teacher, your friends, and your school orchestra.

Teachers, jump in. Even though you may not improvise regularly, *Rockin' Strings* will lead you right along with the students. Be brave! Trust us. You will be safe using *Rockin' Strings* in your string classes and studios. Easy to understand and designed for success, you and your students will now have a way to complement our great classical solo and school orchestra repertoire. *Rockin' Strings* will introduce your students to a new genre of music and creativity, using their string instruments to reinforce the great playing foundation you are giving them. Plus, bringing today's music into your studio or classroom may attract even more attention to strings in your schools and community.

During the last few years we have pilot tested *Rockin' Strings* with over 250 teachers and over 500 intermediate string students. The pedagogy is streamlined, sequential, with unison melodies, duets, and arrangements, all incorporating a carefully structured sequence for learning how to improvise successfully for both you and your students. This gives students the opportunity to create their own music through improvisation, transfer their playing skills from classical to improvising and back again, develop independent musicianship, and have some fun – while getting even more excited about playing a string instrument.

Teachers of all different backgrounds have found success with *Rockin' Strings*. I am confident that you will, too. I strongly support the work of Mark Wood and *Rockin' Strings*. Mark has introduced me to the world of improvising with rock 'n' roll music, and I have had the pleasure of bringing string pedagogy for students to Mark. As a music educator, I was happy to contribute some musical advice to this publication.

Are you ready for new musical experiences? Grab your instrument. Turn on the audio tracks and get started. The world of today's music, along with making your own, is waiting for you. *Rockin' Strings* is the door. Open it and get flying!

Dr. Robert Gillespie, violinist
Professor of Music, Ohio State University
Co-author, *Essential Elements for Strings*
publ. Hal Leonard Corporation

INTRODUCTION

How to Use This Book

This method introduces a set of improvisational adventures designed to explore the wondrous world of your students' imagination and their interaction with music making. Each stage in the book builds on the progression of the learning curve, from easy to more challenging.

It is important that we teach improvising. Not only is it required in the National Standards of Music Teaching, but it also empowers the student to "find" themselves in their chosen instrument, enabling the formation of a lifelong bond to the joy of music. If you, the teacher, are new to improvising, we encourage you to participate alongside the students. The call-and-response part of the book is important for additional ear training and for freedom of instantaneous expression. Invent your own melodies to pass back and forth from teacher to student. Since music is a language skill, have a spontaneous musical conversation every day!

Clear intonation and rhythmic accuracy are the two biggest challenges for string players. Recognizing this, the play-along tracks were set up as an ear-empowering exercise. Each track was composed to the highest standards of music production, by adding great live musicians and by a strong commitment to melody. As you approach each etude, always use the play-along tracks, so the students can anchor onto the drone to reinforce intonation and anchor to the loops for rhythmic acuity. It would be a good idea to place all the audio tracks onto an iPad or computer to loop and control each example. Additionally, Hal Leonard's **PLAYBACK+** is a multifunctional audio player that allows you to slow down audio without changing pitch, set loop points, change keys, and pan left or right.

The basic major, minor, pentatonic, and modal scales are covered in this book. As you deem appropriate, share with your students any additional scale information, showing them how to apply the scales to improvisation.

Finally, the last song, "Night Rider," is a performance piece that can be played at any event, showcasing the depth of your students' expression and their commitment to owning the music for themselves. Their voice matters!

I would like to thank Dr. Robert Gillespie for partnering with me on this wonderful project of bringing strings into the 21st century. He is a great musician and truly is the Yoda of string pedagogy. Likewise, I owe a debt of gratitude to Elizabeth Petersen for the cello pedagogy, to Aaron Yackley for the double bass pedagogy, and to everyone at Ohio State University for their support of future string teachers.

–Mark Wood

STAGE 1
The Building Blocks of Improvisation
D Major

BUILDING BLOCKS

1. D Major Scale

2. D Major Arpeggio

3. D Major

4. FOLLOW THE LEADER

Improvisation
Use the rhythm indicated. Choose any notes in the first two measures to play.

5. UNDERCOVER

Improvisation
Use the rhythm indicated. Choose any notes in the first two measures to play.

6. MOVING ON

Improvisation
Use the rhythm indicated. Choose any notes in the first two measures to play.

7. RUN JUMP

Improvisation
Use the rhythm indicated. Choose any notes in the first two measures to play.

8. FEEL THE TWO

Improvisation
Use the rhythm indicated. Choose any notes in the first two measures to play.

9. TWO FOR TWO

Emphasizing beats 2 and 4
Body movement: Rock back and forth with the beat while playing.

10. TWO PLUS FOUR

11. FOUR WITH TWO

12A. TWICE AS FUN (Duet A)

12B. TWICE AS FUN (Duet B)

D Major and B Minor

BUILDING BLOCKS
B Minor Scale

13. STREETS OF NYC
B minor

Improvisation
Use the rhythm indicated. Choose any notes in the first two measures to play.

14. HOME BASE
B minor

Improvisation

15. ONE WHEEL
B minor

Improvisation

16. FAR AND WIDE
B minor

Improvisation

17. CLIMB
D major

Improvisation

18. TALK THE TALK
D major

Improvisation

19. ANSWER
D major

Improvisation

20. VIOLETS ARE BLUE
D major

Improvisation (2 bars)

D Major

G Major

BUILDING BLOCKS
30. G Major Scale

31. G Major Arpeggio

32. FOLLOW THE LEADER   *(Use any rhythm.)*
Improvisation

33. RUN JUMP
Improvisation

34. UNDERCOVER
Improvisation

35. MOVING ON
Improvisation

36. SKATEBOARD FAN
Improvisation

37. FEEL THE TWO
Improvisation

38. TWO FOR TWO
Improvisation

Improvisation

G Major and E Minor

BUILDING BLOCKS
E Minor Scale

39. STREETS OF NYC
E minor

(Use any rhythm.)
Improvisation

40. NIGHT SKY
E minor

Improvisation

41. ONE WHEEL
E minor

Improvisation

42. FAR AND WIDE
E minor

Improvisation

43. GOING HOME
G major

Improvisation

44. TALK THE TALK
G major

Improvisation

45. ANSWER
G major

Improvisation

46. STRUT
G major

Improvisation (2 bars)

47. WALK THAT WAY
G major

Improvisation

Improvisation

C Major

C Major and A Minor

BUILDING BLOCKS
A Minor Scale

57. EYES ARE DEEP
A minor

(Use any rhythm.)
Improvisation

58. RAIN
A minor

Improvisation

59. GLIMMER
A minor

Improvisation

60. FAR AND WIDE
A minor

Improvisation

61. SUNRISE
C major

Improvisation

62. TALK THE TALK
C major

Improvisation

63. ANSWER
C major

Improvisation

64. VIOLETS ARE BLUE
C major

Improvisation (2 bars)

A Major

A Major and F♯ Minor

BUILDING BLOCKS
F♯ Minor Scale

74. SNOW FOX
F♯ minor
Improvisation

75. OIL AND WATER
F♯ minor
Improvisation

76. FAR AND WIDE
F♯ minor
Improvisation

77. DARK TO LIGHT
F♯ minor
Improvisation

78. ONE WHEEL
A major
Improvisation

79. ANSWER
A major
Improvisation

80. KICK START
A major
Improvisation

81. VIOLETS ARE BLUE
A major
Improvisation (2 bars)

STAGE 2
Intervals

OCTAVES
82. ON ALL STRINGS

83. OCTAVES WITH 8th NOTES

84. SKIP JUMP

85. INTERVALS

5th   4th   3rd   2nd   6th   7th   octave

86. G MAJOR SCALE IN THIRDS

87. G MAJOR SCALE IN FOURTHS

88. G MAJOR SCALE IN FIFTHS

STAGE 3
Major Pentatonic Scales with Improvisation

D Major Pentatonic

89. D Major Pentatonic Scale

90. D Major Pentatonic Scale (lowest note to highest note in 1st position)

91. JUMP UP

92. SMILE

93. COUNTRY FEEL

94. STRAW HAT

95. CALL/RESPONSE

G Major Pentatonic

96. G Major Pentatonic Scale

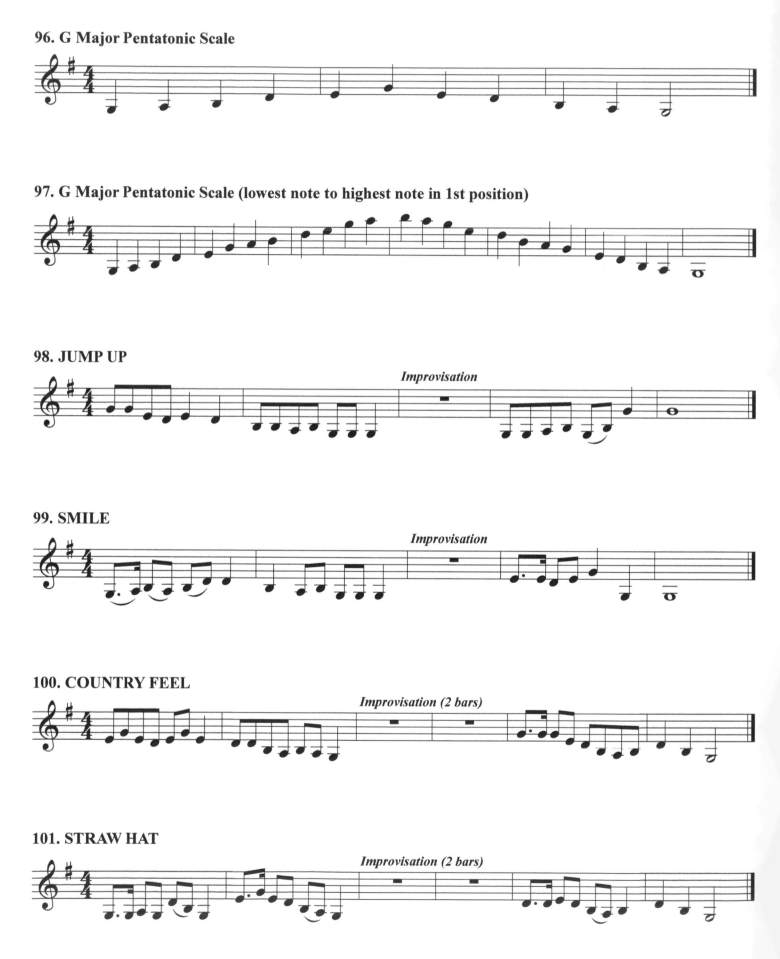

97. G Major Pentatonic Scale (lowest note to highest note in 1st position)

98. JUMP UP

Improvisation

99. SMILE

Improvisation

100. COUNTRY FEEL

Improvisation (2 bars)

101. STRAW HAT

Improvisation (2 bars)

C Major Pentatonic

102. C Major Pentatonic Scale

103. C Major Pentatonic Scale (lowest note to highest note in 1st position)

104. JUMP

Improvisation

105. SMILE

Improvisation

106. COUNTRY FEEL

Improvisation (2 bars)

107. STRAW HAT

Improvisation (2 bars)

A Major Pentatonic

108. A Major Pentatonic Scale

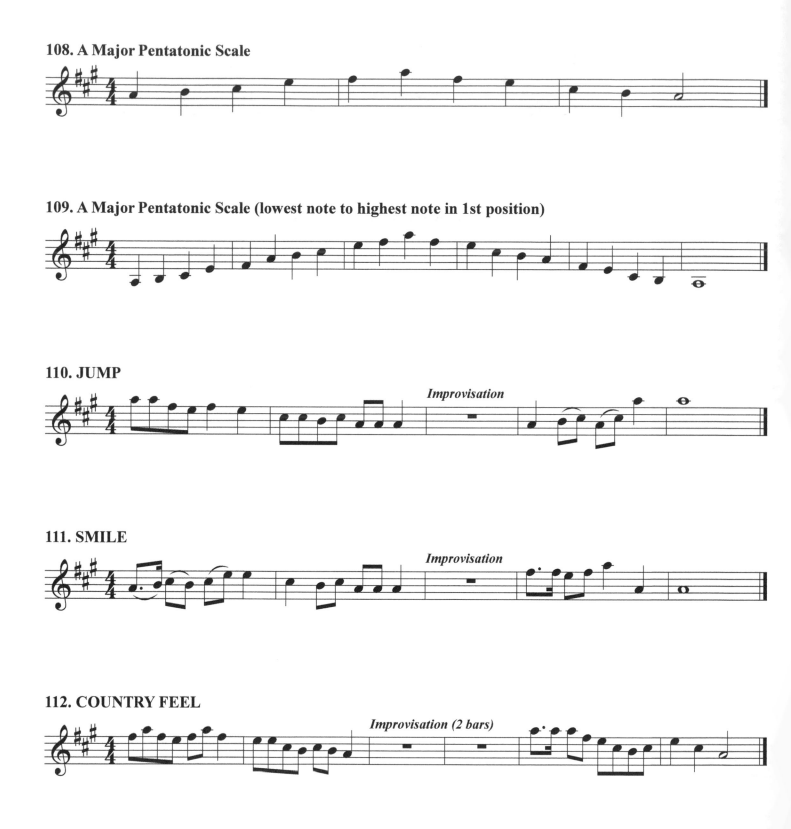

109. A Major Pentatonic Scale (lowest note to highest note in 1st position)

110. JUMP

Improvisation

111. SMILE

Improvisation

112. COUNTRY FEEL

Improvisation (2 bars)

113. STRAW HAT

Improvisation (2 bars)

Syncopation

114. CALL AND RESPONSE

STAGE 4
Learning to Fly in D Major

MUSICAL TOOL KIT TO CREATE YOUR OWN MUSIC
D Major Pentatonic Scale

Rhythmic Ideas

115. LEARNING TO FLY (2-bar solo)

Improvisation (2 bars)
(Choose any notes and rhythms from
the first two lines at the top of the page.)

116. LEARNING TO FLY (4-bar solo)

(harmonic note on A string)

Improvisation (4 bars)
(Choose any notes and rhythms from the first two lines at the top of the page.)

Learning to Fly in G Major

MUSICAL TOOL KIT TO CREATE YOUR OWN MUSIC
G Major Pentatonic Scale

Rhythmic Ideas

117. LEARNING TO FLY (2-bar solo)

Improvisation (2 bars)
(Choose any notes and rhythms from
the first two lines at the top of the page.)

118. LEARNING TO FLY (4-bar solo)

Improvisation (4 bars)
(Choose any notes and rhythms from the first two lines at the top of the page.)

(harmonic note on D string)

Learning to Fly in C Major

MUSICAL TOOL KIT TO CREATE YOUR OWN MUSIC
C Major Pentatonic Scale

Rhythmic Ideas

119. LEARNING TO FLY (2-bar solo)

Improvisation (2 bars)
(Choose any notes and rhythms from the first two lines at the top of the page.)

120. LEARNING TO FLY (4-bar solo)

Improvisation (4 bars)
(Choose any notes and rhythms from the first two lines at the top of the page.)

Learning to Fly in A Major

MUSICAL TOOL KIT TO CREATE YOUR OWN MUSIC
A Major Pentatonic Scale

Rhythmic Ideas

121. LEARNING TO FLY (2-bar solo)

Improvisation (2 bars)
(Choose any notes and rhythms from the first two lines at the top of the page.)

122. LEARNING TO FLY (4-bar solo)

(harmonic note on E string)

Improvisation (4 bars)
(Choose any notes and rhythms from the first two lines at the top of the page.)

STAGE 5
Flying in D Major

D Major Pentatonic Scale

123. FLYING

Improv with the D major pentatonic scale.
Choose your notes from the scale at the top of page 24.
Use any rhythms you want when you improv.

Flying in G Major

G Major Pentatonic Scale

124. FLYING

Improv with the G major pentatonic scale.
Choose your notes from the scale at the top of page 26.
Use any rhythms you want when you improv.

Improv with the G major pentatonic scale.
Choose your notes from the scale at the top of page 26.
Use any rhythms you want when you improv.

Flying in C Major

C Major Pentatonic Scale

125. FLYING

Improv with the C major pentatonic scale.
Choose your notes from the scale at the top of page 28.
Use any rhythms you want when you improv.

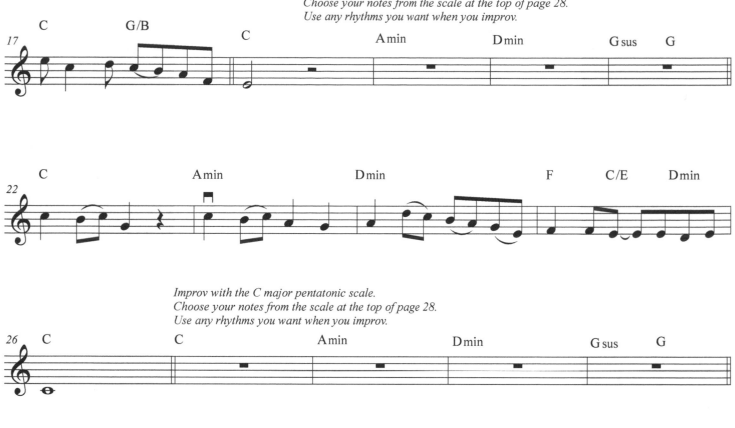

Improv with the C major pentatonic scale.
Choose your notes from the scale at the top of page 28.
Use any rhythms you want when you improv.

Flying in A Major

A Major Pentatonic Scale

126. FLYING

Improv with the A major pentatonic scale.
Choose your notes from the scale at the top of page 30.
Use any rhythms you want when you improv.

Improv with the A major pentatonic scale.
Choose your notes from the scale at the top of page 30.
Use any rhythms you want when you improv.

STAGE 6
Pentatonic Scales & Blues Scales
B Minor Pentatonic/Blues Scales

127. B Minor Pentatonic Scale

128. B Minor Pentatonic Scale (lowest note to highest note in 1st position)

129. DEEP THOUGHT

Improvisation

130. STEP BY STEP

Improvisation

131. DOWN AND UP

Improvisation

132. REACH THE TOP

Improvisation

133. B Minor Blues Scale

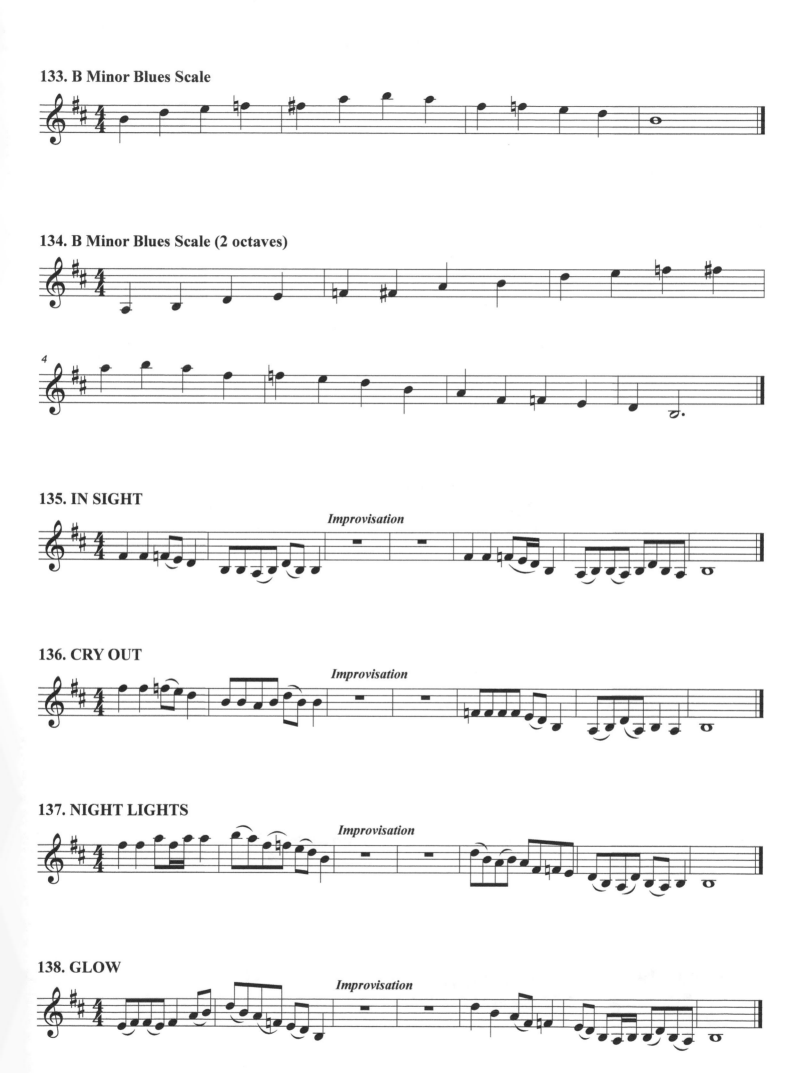

134. B Minor Blues Scale (2 octaves)

135. IN SIGHT

Improvisation

136. CRY OUT

Improvisation

137. NIGHT LIGHTS

Improvisation

138. GLOW

Improvisation

E Minor Pentatonic/Blues Scales

139. E Minor Pentatonic Scale

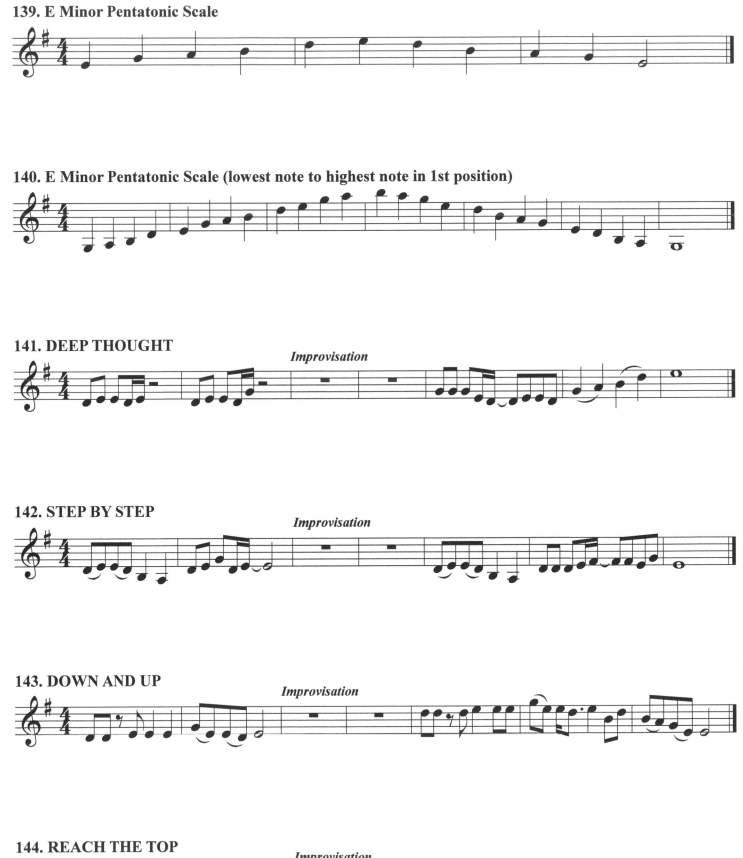

140. E Minor Pentatonic Scale (lowest note to highest note in 1st position)

141. DEEP THOUGHT

Improvisation

142. STEP BY STEP

Improvisation

143. DOWN AND UP

Improvisation

144. REACH THE TOP

Improvisation

145. E Minor Blues Scale

146. E Minor Blues Scale (2 octaves)

147. IN SIGHT

Improvisation

148. CRY OUT

Improvisation

149. NIGHT LIGHTS

Improvisation

150. GLOW

Improvisation

A Minor Pentatonic/Blues Scales

151. A Minor Pentatonic Scale

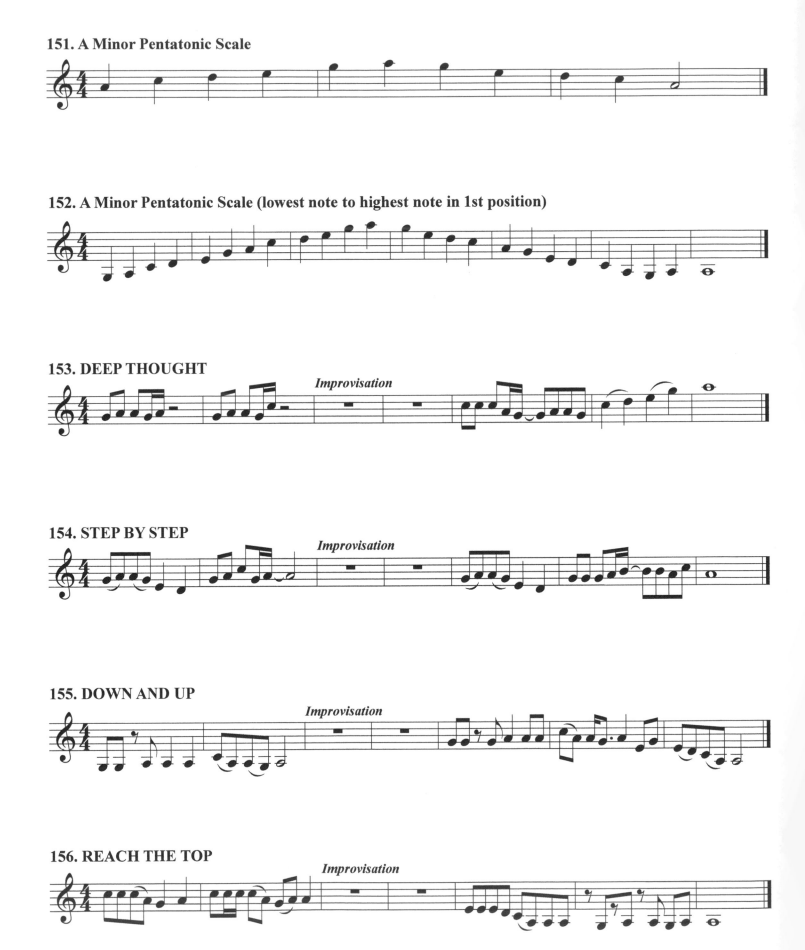

152. A Minor Pentatonic Scale (lowest note to highest note in 1st position)

153. DEEP THOUGHT

Improvisation

154. STEP BY STEP

Improvisation

155. DOWN AND UP

Improvisation

156. REACH THE TOP

Improvisation

157. A Minor Blues Scale

158. A Minor Blues Scale (2 octaves)

4

159. IN SIGHT

Improvisation

160. CRY OUT

Improvisation

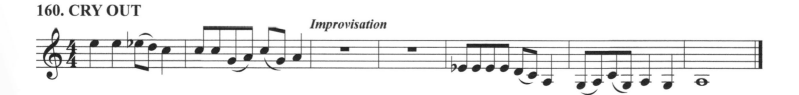

161. NIGHT LIGHTS

Improvisation

162. GLOW

Improvisation

F# Minor Pentatonic/Blues Scales

163. F# Minor Pentatonic Scale

164. F# Minor Pentatonic Scale (lowest note to highest note in 1st position)

165. DEEP THOUGHT

Improvisation

166. STEP BY STEP

Improvisation

167. DOWN AND UP

Improvisation

168. REACH THE TOP

Improvisation

169. F# Minor Blues Scale

170. F# Minor Blues Scale (2 octaves)

171. IN SIGHT

Improvisation

172. CRY OUT

Improvisation

173. NIGHT LIGHTS

Improvisation

174. GLOW

Improvisation

STAGE 7
Blues Shuffle in A Minor

A Minor Blues Scale

175. Blues Shuffle with Triplets

12-bar blues chords

STAGE 8
Night Rider

By Mark Wood

Violin I

Improv using the A min pentatonic scale

STAGE 8
Night Rider

Violin II

By Mark Wood

Night Rider

By Mark Wood

Improv using the A min pentatonic scale

ABOUT THE AUTHOR

Photo by Maryanne Bilham

Recording artist, performer, producer, inventor, Emmy-winning composer and music education advocate Mark Wood has spent the past four decades electrifying the orchestra industry – literally.

Dubbed "The Les Paul of the Violin World" by PBS, the Juilliard-trained violinist first turned the string establishment on its head in the early 1970s with his invention of the first solid-body electric violin. His company, Wood Violins, is the premier manufacturer of electric violins, violas, and cellos worldwide. Mark holds the patent for the first-ever self-supporting violin.

Wood is a world-renowned performer who rose to fame as string master and founding member of the internationally acclaimed Trans-Siberian Orchestra. A successful solo artist in his own right, Wood writes and records original music for film and television, has released six solo albums, and tours with his band The Mark Wood Experience (MWE), which features his wife, vocalist Laura Kaye, and their drummer son Elijah. His commission credits include The Juilliard School and extensive TV broadcast music including The Winter Olympics and The Tour de France (for which he won an Emmy).

In addition to his continued solo and commission work, Wood has collaborated with and appeared alongside some of the biggest names in music, such as Lenny Kravitz, Celine Dion, and Kanye West. As a member of his touring band, Wood had the honor of performing with the legendary Billy Joel for both historic final concerts at Shea stadium, sharing the stage with Paul McCartney, Steven Tyler, and Roger Daltry. He also starred in a Kanye West-produced national Pepsi TV commercial and has appeared on the world's most venerable stages, including Carnegie Hall, Lincoln Center, and Madison Square Garden.

But his true passion is music education. His program Electrify Your Strings (EYS) – now in its 15th year – is an intensive rock-and-roll workshop for school music education departments that boosts student self-esteem and motivation and helps raise money for music education. Today EYS visits upward of 60 schools per year. The organization has been featured on *The Today Show* and *CBS Evening News* and in countless local media outlets.

But for Wood, it's all about the kids. He's dedicated to providing educators with the opportunity to ignite their students' passions and to inspiring students to open their minds and unlock their potential. His book *Electrify Your Strings: The Mark Wood Improvisational Violin Method* is regarded as the definitive electric violin method book. The first in a series of forthcoming educational books, Wood is passionate about providing educators and students with the tools they need to succeed in the classroom and beyond.

101 SONGS

BIG COLLECTIONS OF FAVORITE SONGS ARRANGED FOR SOLO INSTRUMENTALISTS.

101 BROADWAY SONGS

00154199	Flute	$15.99
00154200	Clarinet	$15.99
00154201	Alto Sax	$15.99
00154202	Tenor Sax	$16.99
00154203	Trumpet	$15.99
00154204	Horn	$15.99
00154205	Trombone	$15.99
00154206	Violin	$15.99
00154207	Viola	$15.99
00154208	Cello	$15.99

101 DISNEY SONGS

00244104	Flute	$17.99
00244106	Clarinet	$17.99
00244107	Alto Sax	$17.99
00244108	Tenor Sax	$17.99
00244109	Trumpet	$17.99
00244112	Horn	$17.99
00244120	Trombone	$17.99
00244121	Violin	$17.99
00244125	Viola	$17.99
00244126	Cello	$17.99

101 MOVIE HITS

00158087	Flute	$15
00158088	Clarinet	$15
00158089	Alto Sax	$15
00158090	Tenor Sax	$15
00158091	Trumpet	$15
00158092	Horn	$15
00158093	Trombone	$15
00158094	Violin	$15
00158095	Viola	$15
00158096	Cello	$15

101 CHRISTMAS SONGS

00278637	Flute	$15.99
00278638	Clarinet	$15.99
00278639	Alto Sax	$15.99
00278640	Tenor Sax	$15.99
00278641	Trumpet	$15.99
00278642	Horn	$14.99
00278643	Trombone	$15.99
00278644	Violin	$15.99
00278645	Viola	$15.99
00278646	Cello	$15.99

101 HIT SONGS

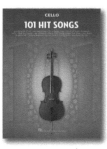

00194561	Flute	$17.99
00197182	Clarinet	$17.99
00197183	Alto Sax	$17.99
00197184	Tenor Sax	$17.99
00197185	Trumpet	$17.99
00197186	Horn	$17.99
00197187	Trombone	$17.99
00197188	Violin	$17.99
00197189	Viola	$17.99
00197190	Cello	$17.99

101 POPULAR SONGS

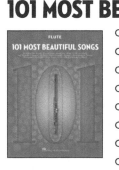

00224722	Flute	$17
00224723	Clarinet	$17
00224724	Alto Sax	$17
00224725	Tenor Sax	$17
00224726	Trumpet	$17
00224727	Horn	$17
00224728	Trombone	$17
00224729	Violin	$17
00224730	Viola	$17
00224731	Cello	$17

101 CLASSICAL THEMES

00155315	Flute	$15.99
00155317	Clarinet	$15.99
00155318	Alto Sax	$15.99
00155319	Tenor Sax	$15.99
00155320	Trumpet	$15.99
00155321	Horn	$15.99
00155322	Trombone	$15.99
00155323	Violin	$15.99
00155324	Viola	$15.99
00155325	Cello	$15.99

101 JAZZ SONGS

00146363	Flute	$15.99
00146364	Clarinet	$15.99
00146366	Alto Sax	$15.99
00146367	Tenor Sax	$15.99
00146368	Trumpet	$15.99
00146369	Horn	$14.99
00146370	Trombone	$15.99
00146371	Violin	$15.99
00146372	Viola	$15.99
00146373	Cello	$15.99

101 MOST BEAUTIFUL SON

00291023	Flute	$
00291041	Clarinet	$
00291042	Alto Sax	$
00291043	Tenor Sax	$
00291044	Trumpet	$
00291045	Horn	$
00291046	Trombone	$
00291047	Violin	$
00291048	Viola	$
00291049	Cello	$

See complete song lists and sample pages at www.halleonard.com

HAL•LEONARD INSTRUMENTAL PLAY-ALONG

Your favorite songs are arranged just for solo instrumentalists with this outstanding series. Each book includes great full-accompaniment play-along audio so you can sound just like a pro!

Check out **halleonard.com** for songlists and more titles!

12 Pop Hits
12 songs
00261790	Flute	00261795	Horn
00261791	Clarinet	00261796	Trombone
00261792	Alto Sax	00261797	Violin
00261793	Tenor Sax	00261798	Viola
00261794	Trumpet	00261799	Cello

The Very Best of Bach
15 selections
00225371	Flute	00225376	Horn
00225372	Clarinet	00225377	Trombone
00225373	Alto Sax	00225378	Violin
00225374	Tenor Sax	00225379	Viola
00225375	Trumpet	00225380	Cello

The Beatles
15 songs
00225330	Flute	00225335	Horn
00225331	Clarinet	00225336	Trombone
00225332	Alto Sax	00225337	Violin
00225333	Tenor Sax	00225338	Viola
00225334	Trumpet	00225339	Cello

Chart Hits
12 songs
00146207	Flute	00146212	Horn
00146208	Clarinet	00146213	Trombone
00146209	Alto Sax	00146214	Violin
00146210	Tenor Sax	00146211	Trumpet
00146216	Cello		

Christmas Songs
12 songs
00146855	Flute	00146863	Horn
00146858	Clarinet	00146864	Trombone
00146859	Alto Sax	00146866	Violin
00146860	Tenor Sax	00146867	Viola
00146862	Trumpet	00146868	Cello

Contemporary Broadway
15 songs
00298704	Flute	00298709	Horn
00298705	Clarinet	00298710	Trombone
00298706	Alto Sax	00298711	Violin
00298707	Tenor Sax	00298712	Viola
00298708	Trumpet	00298713	Cello

Disney Movie Hits
12 songs
00841420	Flute	00841424	Horn
00841687	Oboe	00841425	Trombone
00841421	Clarinet	00841426	Violin
00841422	Alto Sax	00841427	Viola
00841686	Tenor Sax	00841428	Cello
00841423	Trumpet		

Prices, contents, and availability subject to change without notice.

...ney characters and artwork ™ & © 2021 Disney

Disney Solos
12 songs
00841404	Flute	00841506	Oboe
00841406	Alto Sax	00841409	Trumpet
00841407	Horn	00841410	Violin
00841411	Viola	00841412	Cello
00841405	Clarinet/Tenor Sax		
00841408	Trombone/Baritone		
00841553	Mallet Percussion		

Dixieland Favorites
15 songs
00268756	Flute	0068759	Trumpet
00268757	Clarinet	00268760	Trombone
00268758	Alto Sax		

Billie Eilish
9 songs
00345648	Flute	00345653	Horn
00345649	Clarinet	00345654	Trombone
00345650	Alto Sax	00345655	Violin
00345651	Tenor Sax	00345656	Viola
00345652	Trumpet	00345657	Cello

Favorite Movie Themes
13 songs
00841166	Flute	00841168	Trumpet
00841167	Clarinet	00841170	Trombone
00841169	Alto Sax	00841296	Violin

Gospel Hymns
15 songs
00194648	Flute	00194654	Trombone
00194649	Clarinet	00194655	Violin
00194650	Alto Sax	00194656	Viola
00194651	Tenor Sax	00194657	Cello
00194652	Trumpet		

Great Classical Themes
15 songs
00292727	Flute	00292733	Horn
00292728	Clarinet	00292735	Trombone
00292729	Alto Sax	00292736	Violin
00292730	Tenor Sax	00292737	Viola
00292732	Trumpet	00292738	Cello

The Greatest Showman
8 songs
00277389	Flute	00277394	Horn
00277390	Clarinet	00277395	Trombone
00277391	Alto Sax	00277396	Violin
00277392	Tenor Sax	00277397	Viola
00277393	Trumpet	00277398	Cello

Irish Favorites
31 songs
00842489	Flute	00842495	Trombone
00842490	Clarinet	00842496	Violin
00842491	Alto Sax	00842497	Viola
00842493	Trumpet	00842498	Cello
00842494	Horn		

Michael Jackson
11 songs
00119495	Flute	00119499	Trumpet
00119496	Clarinet	00119501	Trombone
00119497	Alto Sax	00119503	Violin
00119498	Tenor Sax	00119502	Accomp.

Jazz & Blues
14 songs
00841438	Flute	00841441	Trumpet
00841439	Clarinet	00841443	Trombone
00841440	Alto Sax	00841444	Violin
00841442	Tenor Sax		

Jazz Classics
12 songs
00151812	Flute	00151816	Trumpet
00151813	Clarinet	00151818	Trombone
00151814	Alto Sax	00151819	Violin
00151815	Tenor Sax	00151821	Cello

Les Misérables
13 songs
00842292	Flute	00842297	Horn
00842293	Clarinet	00842298	Trombone
00842294	Alto Sax	00842299	Violin
00842295	Tenor Sax	00842300	Viola
00842296	Trumpet	00842301	Cello

Metallica
12 songs
02501327	Flute	02502454	Horn
02501339	Clarinet	02501329	Trombone
02501332	Alto Sax	02501334	Violin
02501333	Tenor Sax	02501335	Viola
02501330	Trumpet	02501338	Cello

Motown Classics
15 songs
00842572	Flute	00842576	Trumpet
00842573	Clarinet	00842578	Trombone
00842574	Alto Sax	00842579	Violin
00842575	Tenor Sax		

Pirates of the Caribbean
16 songs
00842183	Flute	00842188	Horn
00842184	Clarinet	00842189	Trombone
00842185	Alto Sax	00842190	Violin
00842186	Tenor Sax	00842191	Viola
00842187	Trumpet	00842192	Cello

Queen
17 songs
00285402	Flute	00285407	Horn
00285403	Clarinet	00285408	Trombone
00285404	Alto Sax	00285409	Violin
00285405	Tenor Sax	00285410	Viola
00285406	Trumpet	00285411	Cello

Simple Songs
14 songs
00249081	Flute	00249087	Horn
00249093	Oboe	00249089	Trombone
00249082	Clarinet	00249090	Violin
00249083	Alto Sax	00249091	Viola
00249084	Tenor Sax	00249092	Cello
00249086	Trumpet	00249094	Mallets

Superhero Themes
14 songs
00363195	Flute	00363200	Horn
00363196	Clarinet	00363201	Trombone
00363197	Alto Sax	00363202	Violin
00363198	Tenor Sax	00363203	Viola
00363199	Trumpet	00363204	Cello

Star Wars
16 songs
00350900	Flute	00350907	Horn
00350913	Oboe	00350908	Trombone
00350903	Clarinet	00350909	Violin
00350904	Alto Sax	00350910	Viola
00350905	Tenor Sax	00350911	Cello
00350906	Trumpet	00350914	Mallet

Taylor Swift
15 songs
00842532	Flute	00842537	Horn
00842533	Clarinet	00842538	Trombone
00842534	Alto Sax	00842539	Violin
00842535	Tenor Sax	00842540	Viola
00842536	Trumpet	00842541	Cello

Video Game Music
13 songs
00283877	Flute	00283883	Horn
00283878	Clarinet	00283884	Trombone
00283879	Alto Sax	00283885	Violin
00283880	Tenor Sax	00283886	Viola
00283882	Trumpet	00283887	Cello

Wicked
13 songs
00842236	Flute	00842241	Horn
00842237	Clarinet	00842242	Trombone
00842238	Alto Sax	00842243	Violin
00842239	Tenor Sax	00842244	Viola
00842240	Trumpet	00842245	Cello

HAL•LEONARD®

HAL•LEONARD®
VIOLIN
PLAY-ALONG

AUDIO
ACCESS
INCLUDED

The Violin
Play-Along Series
Play your favorite songs quickly and easily!

Just follow the music, listen to the CD or online audio to hear how the violin should sound, and then play along using the separate backing tracks. The audio files are enhanced so you can adjust the recordings to any tempo without changing pitch!

HAL•LEONARD®
www.halleonard.com